GRAPHIC GRATITUDE GUIDES FOR A PRACTICE OF GRATITUDE

BY ETTA JOHNSON

RoseDog Books

PITTSBURGH, PENNSYLVANIA 15238

RoseDog Books
585 Alpha Drive, Suite 103
Pittsburgh, PA 15238
Visit our website at *www.rosedogbookstore.com*

ISBN: 978-1-6495-7934-8
eISBN: 978-1-6495-7955-3

GRAPHIC GRATITUDE GUIDES

for a practice of gratitude

GRATITUDE EXPLORER GUIDE FOR PARENT & CHILD (1½ - 5 years)

GRATITUDE GUIDE FOR KIDS & FAMILIES

GRATITUDE GUIDE FOR ENGLISH LEARNERS

YOUNG ADULT GRATITUDE GUIDE

GRATITUDE GUIDE FOR ADULTS

GRATITUDE GUIDE FOR ELDERS

GRATITUDE FOR KINDNESS

GROWING HOPE, NATURAL GRATITUDE

MORAL COMPASS - THE GOLDEN RULE

THANKFUL FOR THE USA

Etta Johnson 2020

INTRODUCTION:

Why gratitude? I firmly believe that focusing on gratitude results in a positive outlook, a healthy view of life and above all, hope. Living in this unique era of COVID-19, inequity challenges and extreme climatic events, I find that focusing on gratitude for the good things in my life is crucial. Then the bad news balances with good - my blessings.

Research studies show that gratitude improves physical and psychological health, enhances empathy and reduces aggression.

As I became mindful of blessings in different aspects of my life, a mindfulness approach in a graphic format evolved. The Graphic Gratitude Guides are designed for developing a practice of gratitude.   EJ

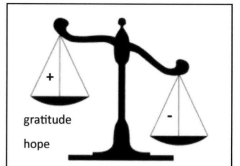

The benefits of gratitude

You feel **hope**, not despair

You have a **positive** attitude, not negative

You have a **bright** outlook, not dark

You feel **glad**, not sad

You focus on **good**, not bad

You feel **lucky**, not unlucky

You are **healthy**, not unhealthy

You are **up**, not down

You help others instead of feeling helpless

You recognize **opportunity** instead of adversity

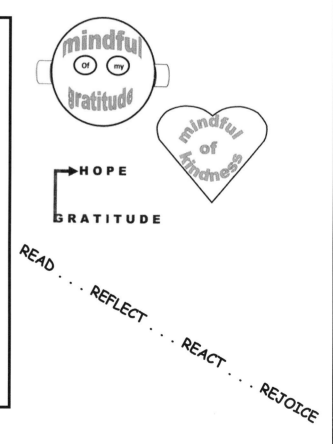

TABLE OF CONTENTS

page

GRATITUDE EXPLORER GUIDE FOR PARENT & CHILD (1 ½ to 5 years) ———————————— 4 - 6

GRATITUDE GUIDE FOR KIDS & FAMILIES ———————————————————————— 7 - 10

GRATITUDE GUIDE FOR ENGLISH LEARNERS ——————————————————————— 11- 13

YOUNG ADULT GRATITUDE GUIDE ——————————————————————————— 14 - 16

GRATITUDE GUIDE FOR ADULTS ——————————————————————————— 17 - 19

GRATITUDE GUIDE FOR ELDERS ——————————————————————————— 20 - 23

MINDFUL OF KINDNESS ————————————————————————————— 24 - 25

NATURAL GRATITUDE ——————————————————————————————— 26

GROWING HOPE ————————————————————————————————— 27

MORAL COMPASS - THE GOLDEN RULE ——————————————————————— 28

THANKFUL FOR THE USA ————————————————————————————— 29

GRATITUDE EXPLORER GUIDE FOR PARENT & CHILD (1½ to 5 years)

gratitude building blocks for talk and play

I can see. I can hear. I can smell. I can taste. I can feel. I can laugh. I am kind.

Look at building block pictures together. Talk about the components in each picture. Then talk about how this relates to your life. What do you see, hear, feel, smell, taste? How do you feel? Model expressing gratitude. (I'm glad, grateful, lucky)

GRATITUDE EXPLORER GUIDE FOR PARENT & CHILD

GRATITUDE EXPLORER CARDS

Directions: Cut out the interlocking gratitude blocks. Laminate or glue onto stiff paper or cardboard & cover with clear contact paper. Encourage your child to play with the cards Talk about how the picture relates to your own life ⬥your home, your family, your activities, routines, view of nature. Model gratitude by telling what you are grateful for.

5

GRATITUDE EXPLORER GUIDE FOR PARENT & CHILD - MY OWN GRATITUDE PICTURES

Talk with your child about what we are grateful for. Encourage your child to draw pictures of his life here.

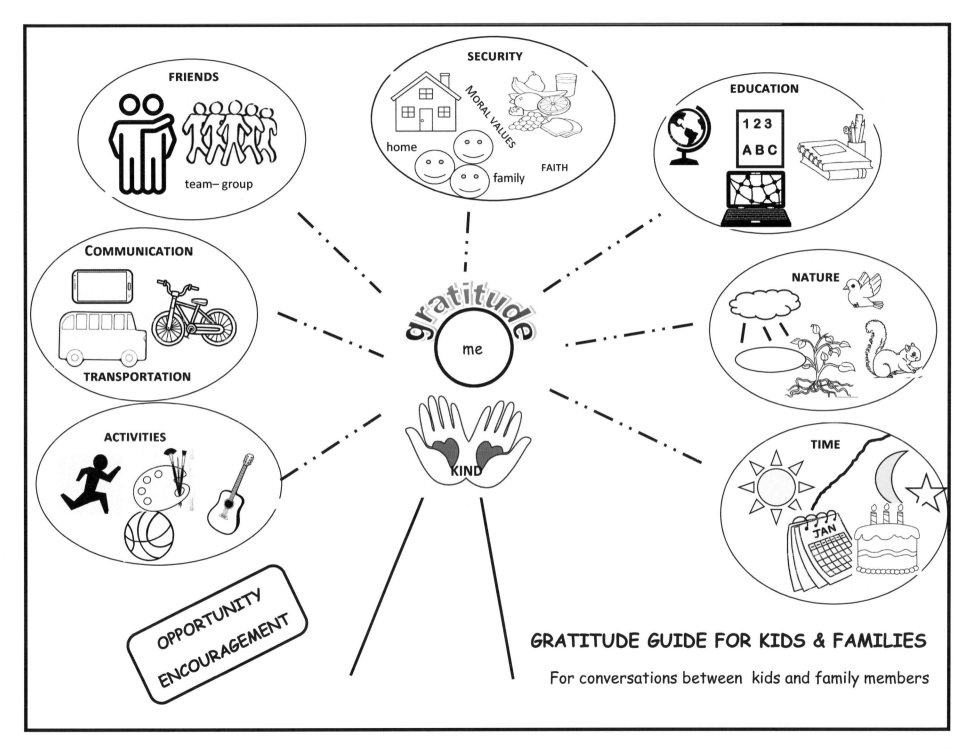

FRIENDS

team–group

SECURITY

MORAL VALUES

home

family

FAITH

EDUCATION

1 2 3
A B C

COMMUNICATION

TRANSPORTATION

NATURE

gratitude

me

ACTIVITIES

KIND

TIME

JAN

OPPORTUNITY ENCOURAGEMENT

GRATITUDE GUIDE FOR KIDS & FAMILIES

For conversations between kids and family members

GRATITUDE GUIDE FOR KIDS & FAMILIES

GRATITUDE HOLDER

GRATITUDE HOLDER
FOR GRATITUDE NOTES

Use this as a family activity or by yourself.

Grip gratitude. Grin with gratitude.

When things go wrong, look for what goes right.

When everything appears dark, look for the light.

Positive +, not negative –. Opportunity, not adversity.

REUSE. Make a simple gratitude holder. Find a clean, empty round container.

Cut scrap paper into strips. Find an old pencil, marker or crayon for writing.

READ. Discuss the pictures on the GRATITUDE GUIDE FOR KIDS & FAMILIES.

REFLECT. What are you grateful for today?

RECORD. Write a gratitude note on a strip of paper.

RETAIN. Put the gratitude notes in the gratitude holder to keep.

REVIEW. Review the gratitude notes.

REPORT. You can collect all the notes into a gratitude report.

REPEAT. Do this daily, weekly, set your own schedule.

GRATITUDE GUIDE FOR KIDS & FAMILIES

GRATITUDE LOG

Keeping a gratitude log is a heathy mindfulness practice. Do this daily, weekly, set your own schedule.

Keep a personal log or a parent and kid log.

<u>CONNECT.</u> Use the picture cues in the GRATITUDE GUIDE FOR KIDS & FAMILIES to focus. What are you grateful for? What do you feel lucky to have? What are you blessed with?

Me: Identity Who am I?

Security: home, family, food, moral values, faith

(Parents, teachers, mentors provide opportunities and encouragement.)

Friends: good friends, family friends, groups, teams, community, empathy

Communication: phone, computer, e-mail, Zoom, TV, direct interaction;

Transportation: car, bus, bike, skate, walk

Education: teacher, classmates, read, write, math, science, social studies, in-school - virtual learning

Activities: sports, music, art, dance, drama, games, chores, cook

Time: day & night, calendar, past-present-future, celebrations, goals

Nature: sun, moon, sky, clouds-rain-water, land & sea, plants & animals, farms

<u>REFLECT.</u> Close your eyes. Visualize.

today	today

<u>RECORD.</u> Express your gratitude in writing. Write today's date and what you are grateful for.

GRATITUDE GUIDE FOR KIDS & FAMILIES

VINDY, A SINGLE, IMMIGRANT MOM KEEPS A GRATITUDE LOG IN VERSE

Today I am grateful . . .

For a roof over our heads,
Kitchen, bathroom, TV, beds.
    That our family is together,
    So any storms we can weather.
For a way to obtain food,
To feed my hungry brood.
    For the faith that keeps me strong,
    Protecting my family from harm.
To connect with kin at home
In the nation I come from.
    To teach my children that equality
    Is a right for people globally.
That empathy is of great importance
For anyone who has real problems.

For a chance to be outside
To see sun and moon and sky,
    Where my kids can play and thrive,
    Part of nature's grand beehive.
For the pandemic's earth-healing deed -
Less pollution from less movement, speed.
    To live in the present, not future or past
    Mindful of every event, connection and task.
So, together daily we can pray,
Thanking God for each new day.

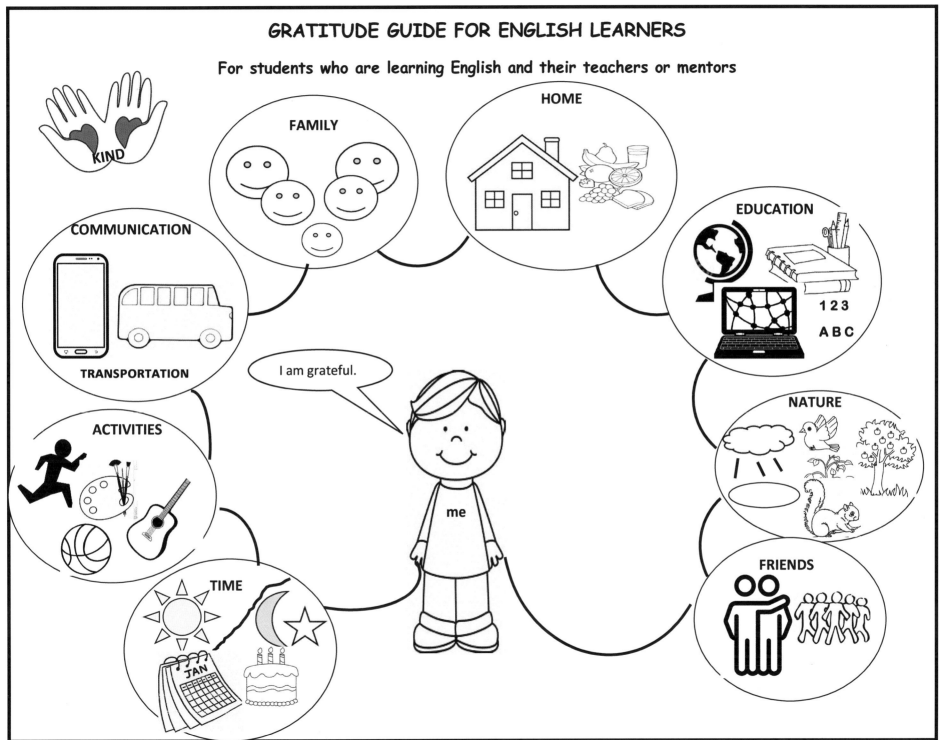

GRATITUDE GUIDE FOR ENGLISH LEARNERS

For students who are learning English and their teachers or mentors

GRATITUDE GUIDE FOR ENGLISH LEARNERS

TALK ABOUT GRATITUDE IN MY LIFE

GRATITUDE VOCABULARY:

Gratitude = thanks– I am full of gratitude for ___

Grateful = thanks – i am grateful for ____

Thankful = thanks—I am thankful for ___

Fortunate = lucky - I am fortunate that ___

Lucky = fortunate—I am lucky that ____

Blessed = happy—I am blessed with ___

Appreciate = grateful —I appreciate __

My name is _____

I am_____

Give it to **me**.

You are reading the guide.

This is **your** guide.

Directions: Look at each picture in the guide. Talk about your life. Answer the questions.

ME   Who are you? What is your name? How old are your? Are you a boy or girl? Where were you born? What are you grateful for?

HOME   Where is your home? What is in your home? What do you eat? What are you grateful for?

FAMILY   Who is in your family? Who lives in your home? Who are you grateful for?

COMMUNICATION   How do you talk to family and friends? How do you see family and friends? What are you grateful for?

TRANSPORTATION   Do you ride the bus? Do you have a car? How do you go shopping? What are you grateful for?

FRIENDS   Who are your friends? Who are you grateful for?

ACTIVITIES   What do you like to do? What are you grateful for?

EDUCATION   What do you study? What is your favorite subject? What are you grateful for?

GRATITUDE GUIDE FOR ENGLISH LEARNERS

MY GRATITUDE WORKSHEET

Directions: Fill in the blank.

1. I am thankful that I can _____

2. I am grateful for _____(my family)

3. I am lucky that I can use the phone to _____(communication)

4. I am lucky to have friends like _____ (friends)

5. I appreciate _____ (education)

6. I am grateful that I can_____at night. (time)

7. I am thankful to_____(activities).

8. I am grateful to see_____outside. (nature)

Directions: Match the words that go together. Draw a <u>line._____</u>

1. Nature	phone
2. Home	pals
3. Education	mother
4. Communication	sun
5. Time	A B C
6. Family	play ball
7. Activities	bed
8. Friends	clock

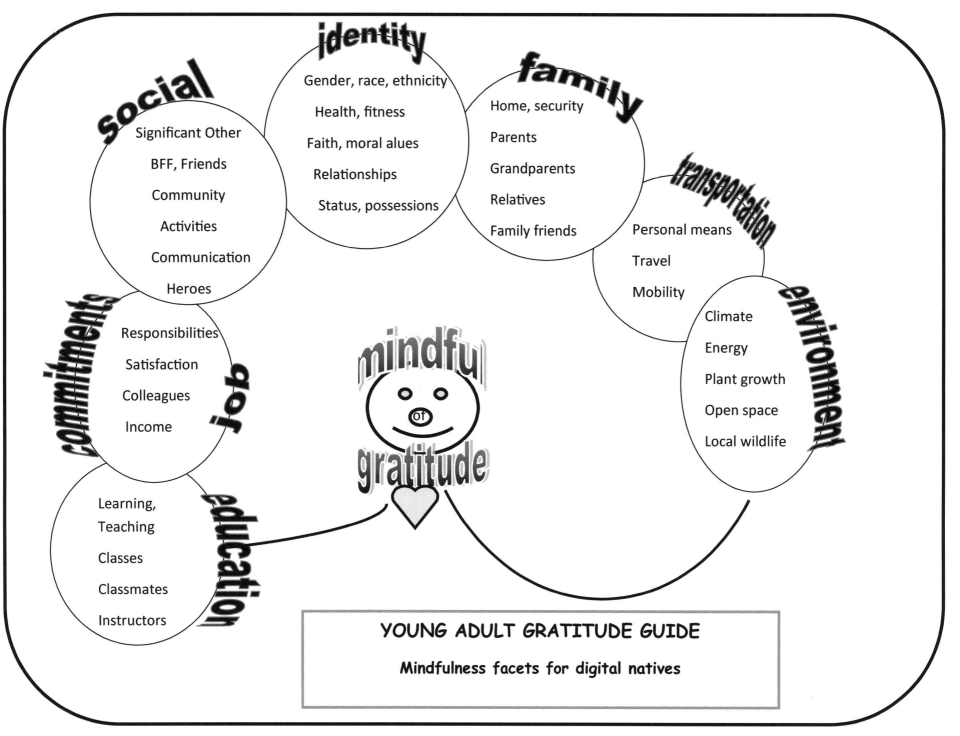

social
- Significant Other
- BFF, Friends
- Community
- Activities
- Communication
- Heroes

identity
- Gender, race, ethnicity
- Health, fitness
- Faith, moral alues
- Relationships
- Status, possessions

family
- Home, security
- Parents
- Grandparents
- Relatives
- Family friends

transportation
- Personal means
- Travel
- Mobility

environment
- Climate
- Energy
- Plant growth
- Open space
- Local wildlife

commitments / job
- Responsibilities
- Satisfaction
- Colleagues
- Income

education
- Learning, Teaching
- Classes
- Classmates
- Instructors

mindful or gratitude

YOUNG ADULT GRATITUDE GUIDE

Mindfulness facets for digital natives

Find a pocket-size notebook in which to record your gratitude on any or all facets.

MINDFUL OF MY
GRATITUDE JOURNAL

Make a practice of writing in your journal regularly.

record mindful of my gratitude moments

PHOTO FILE

As you watch a scene or participate in an event mindfully, record it with your phone.

Make a practice of keeping these in an unshared gratitude file.

POST GRATITUDE

Write something special for which you are grateful on a post-it note. Post on bulletin board, mirror or notebook.

+++++++++++++++++++

Write something special for which you are grateful in a Gratitude folder in Notes on your phone.

MAGNETIC FOODIE GRATITUDE

Reuse scrap paper. Write or sketch a food, drink or meal that you particularly appreciate. Put it on the refrigerator with a magnet.

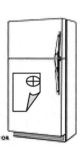

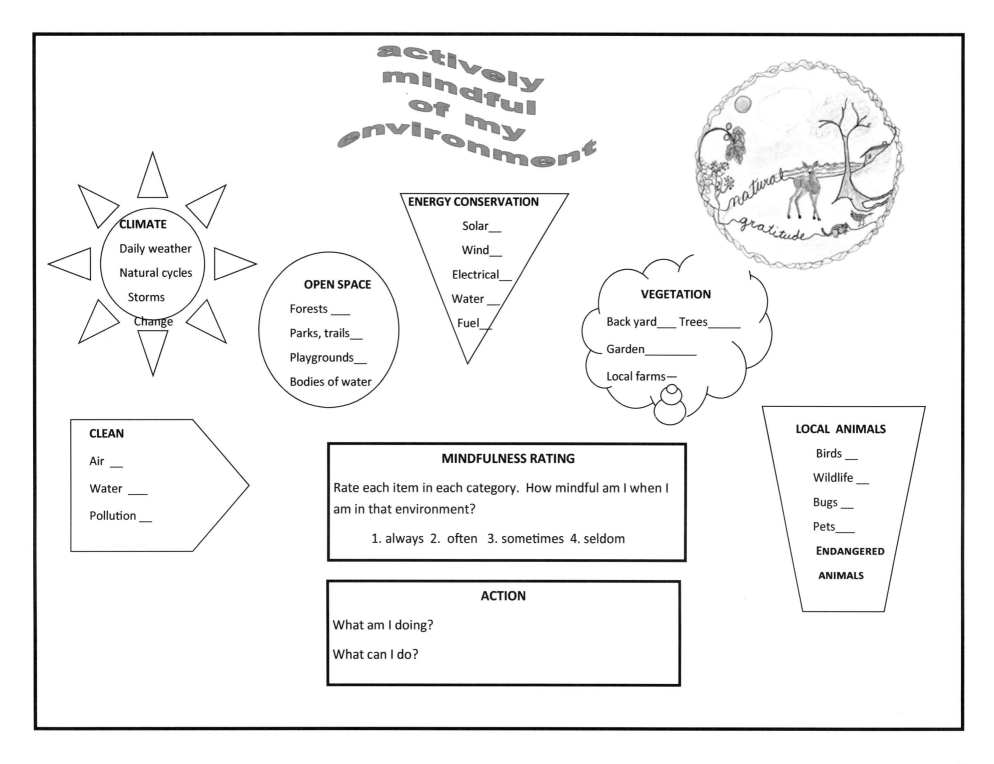

actively mindful of my environment

natural gratitude

CLIMATE

Daily weather

Natural cycles

Storms

Change

OPEN SPACE

Forests ___

Parks, trails__

Playgrounds__

Bodies of water

ENERGY CONSERVATION

Solar__

Wind__

Electrical__

Water __

Fuel__

VEGETATION

Back yard___ Trees_____

Garden_____

Local farms—

CLEAN

Air __

Water ___

Pollution __

MINDFULNESS RATING

Rate each item in each category. How mindful am I when I am in that environment?

1. always 2. often 3. sometimes 4. seldom

ACTION

What am I doing?

What can I do?

LOCAL ANIMALS

Birds __

Wildlife __

Bugs __

Pets___

ENDANGERED

ANIMALS

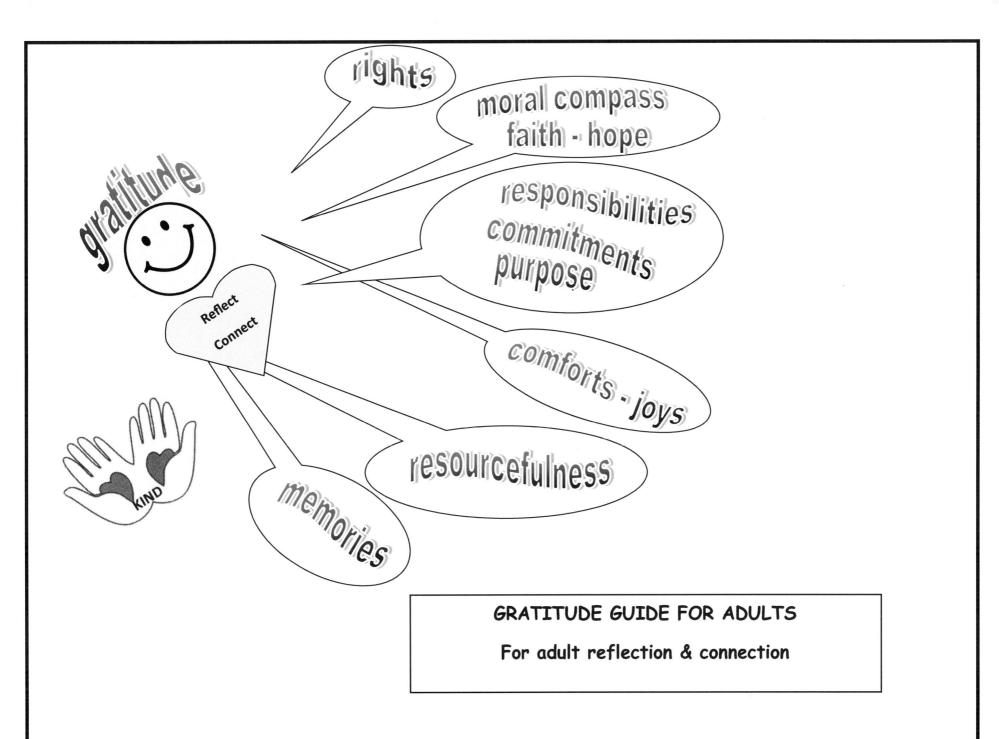

GRATITUDE GUIDE FOR ADULTS

For adult reflection & connection

GRATITUDE GUIDE FOR ADULTS

MY GRATITUDE CHECK-LIST

Objective list of all that I am grateful for

RIGHTS _____

MORAL COMPASS - FAITH - HOPE _____

_____

_____

RESPONSIBILITIES - COMMIGTMENTS - PURPOSE_____

_____

_____

COMFORTS & JOYS _____

RESOURCEFULNESS _____

MEMORIES _____

_____

_____

GRATITUDE GUIDE FOR ADULTS

MY BLESSINGS

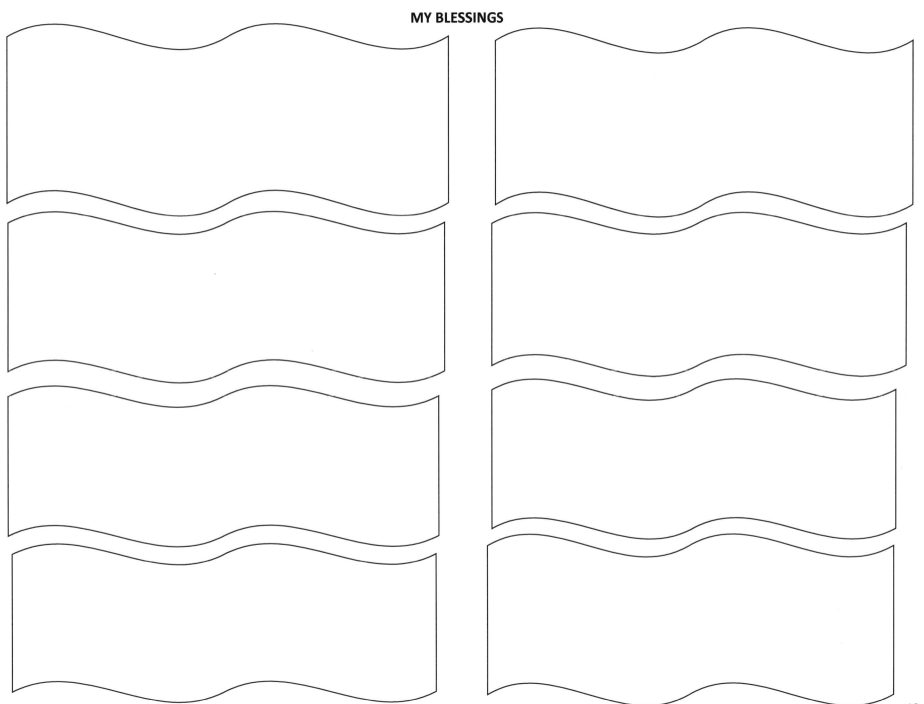

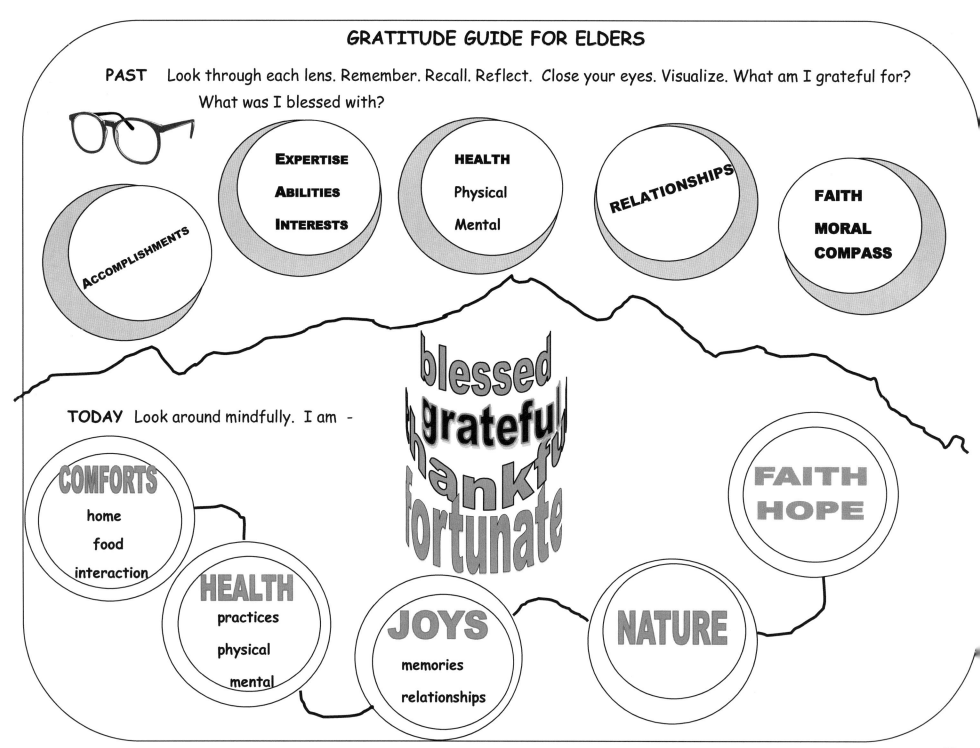

GRATITUDE GUIDE FOR ELDERS

PAST Look through each lens. Remember. Recall. Reflect. Close your eyes. Visualize. What am I grateful for? What was I blessed with?

ACCOMPLISHMENTS

EXPERTISE
ABILITIES
INTERESTS

HEALTH
Physical
Mental

RELATIONSHIPS

FAITH
MORAL
COMPASS

blessed grateful thankful fortunate

TODAY Look around mindfully. I am -

COMFORTS
home
food
interaction

HEALTH
practices
physical
mental

JOYS
memories
relationships

NATURE

FAITH
HOPE

GRATITUDE GUIDE FOR ELDERS

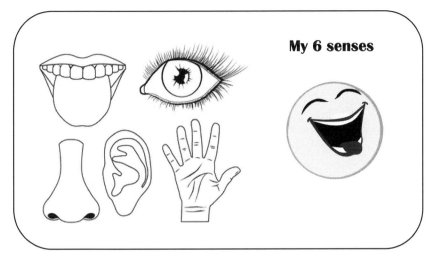

My 6 senses

1. taste 2. sight 3. smell 4. hearing 5. touch 6. humor

GRATITUDE FOR THE SENSE OF HUMOR

Over the course of many years, our six senses become more and more acute and refined.

A baby learns about the world around him by using all his senses, acquires words to communicate what he observes - watching and listening, tasting and touching, smelling and laughing. Then the senses are fine-tuned in childhood.

Over time our senses develop nuances, just as our vocabulary becomes more precisely varied. In our older years, a sense of humor is a saving grace. We are blessed when sensory and spiritual experiences blend.

What tickles your sense of humor? What makes you laugh? What are you grateful for? For which of your senses are you most grateful?

HUMOR JOURNAL

Today's laughs.

GRATITUDE GUIDE FOR ELDERS

MY GRATITUDE MENU

Cook up a menu of gratitude. Visualize cooking meals full of gratitude ingredients. What is on today's Gratitude Menu?

What is on the Past Gratitude Menu? Write both menus, then compare.

PAST GRATITUDE MENU	TODAY'S GRATITUDE MENU
ACCOMPLISHMENTS	**COMFORTS**
EXPERTISE - ABILITIES - INTERESTS	**JOYS**
HEALTH	**HEALTH**
RELATIONSHIPS	**NATURE**
FAITH - MORAL COMPASS	**FAITH - HOPE**

GRATITUDE GUIDE FOR ELDERS
AN ELDER WOMAN"S GRATITUDE EXPRESSED

I am so grateful, I am so blessed . . .

PRESENT

- for eyes to see, ears to hear, a heart to feel and a mind to appreciate the natural beauty all around us

- for the comfort of close family and friends and the joy of each new generation

- for the means and ability to give and the grace to receive, serving others with compassion

- for the faith and hope that give me strength

- for memories that surround and comfort me

PAST

- for a long, loving marriage in a happy home

- for this country which embraced me as a refugee child and allowed me to thrive and teach others

- for my parents who provided me security and the pathway to freedom, and for the creative genes and modeling with which they endowed me

My heart overflows with gratitude.   EJ

++++++++++

SIX SENSES BLESSINGS

I am blessed to be able to use all my <u>six senses</u> naturally.

I am blessed to be able to <u>watch</u> tiny, brown chipmunks scamper on the ground under a canopy of giant rain-enriched green fig leaves.

I am blessed to be able to <u>hear</u> the lilting songs of sparrows, the tap-tapping of woodpeckers, the urgent calls of ravens.

I am blessed to be able to <u>smell</u> the scent of new-mown grass and the blended, fresh aroma wafted around by a gentle breeze.

I am blessed to be able to <u>feel</u> the sun on my skin, the wind in my hair, a pliable honeysuckle vine.

I am blessed to be able to <u>taste</u> a fresh, ripe strawberry; to savor its flavor, after duly admiring its red solidity and perky stem.

I am blessed to be able to <u>laugh</u> at the antics of young squirrels chasing each other up and down and around a tree.

I am blessed to be able to observe minute details and global vistas.

KINDNESS - GIVING

caring smile

listening fully

helpful action

encouraging words

encouraging words

listening ear

helping hand

RECEIVING KINDNESSS

express your gratitude in words, verse, song or any art form

mindful of kindness

KIND

An unexpected kind act

Kind words out of the blue

Surprise gift of something needed

Unanticipated aid

A genuine listener

Unforeseen helping hands

Plain old kindness

BE KIND - ACTS OF KINDNESS

Be kind to someone - in your family, a friend or neighbor, guest or stranger.

When someone is sad, smile and say something nice, make her feel glad.

When someone feels angry, listen, make him feel understood.

When someone is hurt, smile, hug, make her feel better.

When someone has a problem, help him fix it.

When someone looks lonely or lost, give her a smile and helping hand.

You can be kind to someone for no reason at all - just being kind.

Think about your choices. When someone needs help, you can -

- help (unconditional kindness)

- help (conditional kindness - expect something in return)

- ignore (unkind)

PARENTS MODEL & ENCOURAGE KINDNESS

PARENTS ACKNOWLEDGE CHILD'S KINDNESS

I like the way you ___

I'm glad that you are kind to ___

KEEP KINDNESS

KINDNESS CHRONICLE

Personally published weekly – not for distribution

Features acts of kindness—given & received, large & small, private & public.

Cartoons: humorous acts of kindness

Newspaper sections: Kindness received. Generous gestures. kindness given. Kindness that warms the cockles of your heart.

POST KINDNESS QUOTES

A warm smile is the universal language of kindness. ~Ward

Kindness is the language which the deaf can hear and the blind can see.   ~Mark Twain

You cannot do a kindness too soon, for you never know how soon it will be too late.   ~Ralph Waldo Emerson

No act of kindness, no matter how small, is ever wasted.   ~Aesop

Do your little bit of good where you are; it's those little bits of good put together that overwhelm the world.   ~Desmond Tutu

Be kind whenever possible. It is always possible.   ~Dalai   Lama

MY MEMORY BANK

Open all hours

Deposit & save *acts of kindness*

in My Memory Bank

Non-taxable positive assets

No # or PIN to remember

Valuable kindness stocks & bonds

KINDNESS KEEPSAKES

REPURPOSE an old box. Paint, paper, or collage it.

RECALL kindness you have experienced.

COLLECT notes, letters, pictures, mementos to put in the box.

WRITE additional memories to put in the box.

NATURAL GRATITUDE FOR RESIDENT CREATURES GREAT AND SMALL IN OUR HABITAT

resident creatures great & small

Look around outside your home and reflect: -

What are my favorite creatures here?

Which animals am I glad to see?

Which animals do I miss when they aren't around much?

Which animals do I actively nurture?

Which creatures do I feel blessed to be able to watch?

Which creatures communicate with me?

What similarities do I observe between human and animal child rearing behavior??

mindful of my gratitude

residents in our habitat

great and small

deer, foxes, raccoons, groundhogs, rabbits, squirrels, chipmunks, moles
birds - geese, ducks, crows, woodpeckers, song birds

turtles, lizards, snakes, frogs
insects - bees, ants, grasshoppers, ladybugs, butterflies
worms

Co-inhabitants

All things bright and beautiful
All creatures great and small
All things wise and wonderful
The Lord God made them all

GROWING HOPE

Naturally nourished hope blossoms

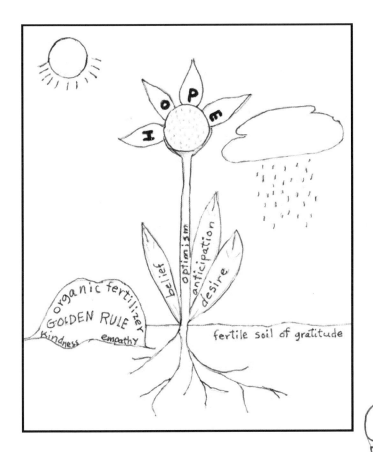

REFLECTIONS ON GROWING HOPE

The roots of hope nestle firmly in the rich soil of gratitude, warmed and energized by the sun, watered with life-giving rain. <u>Reflect</u>: What all am I grateful for? In what is my hope rooted?

When hope is enriched by the organic fertilizer of the Golden Rule, it flourishes. <u>Reflect</u>: How do I nourish hope?

Leaves sprout as the sturdy stem of optimism shoots upward toward the sun. <u>Reflect</u>: Am I generally optimistic?

<u>Reflect on the leaves</u> -

Do I believe that there is hope?

Do I anticipate, look forward to a hopeful future?

Do I truly desire to be hopeful and pass this on to others?

<u>Reflect</u>: How does hope blossom for me?

A MORAL COMPASS

gives directions to

MORAL VALUES - A CODE OF ETHICS

based on THE GOLDEN RULE

Treat others as we wish them to treat us.

Each two-point direction (opposite characteristics)
on the compass is actually a spectrum:

positive   in-between   negative

OUR MORAL VALUES -

-are imparted to our children and others
- are exemplified in our words and deeds
- determine how we conduct our lives
- shape our character

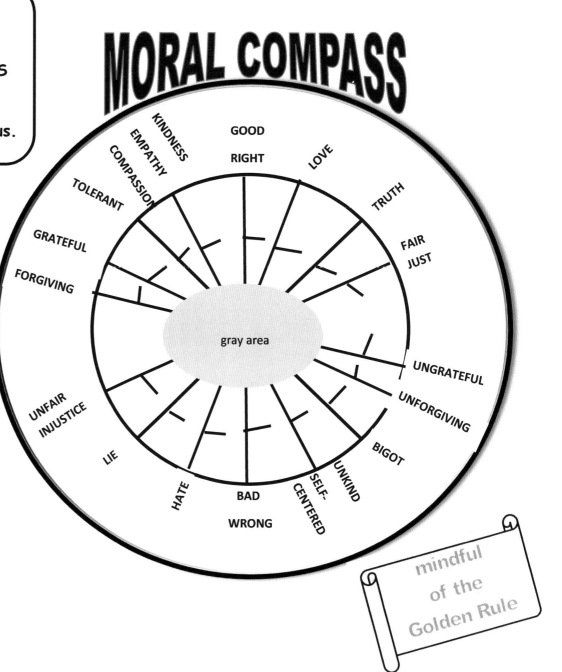

MORAL COMPASS

KINDNESS
EMPATHY
COMPASSION
TOLERANT
GRATEFUL
FORGIVING
GOOD
RIGHT
LOVE
TRUTH
FAIR
JUST
gray area
UNGRATEFUL
UNFORGIVING
BIGOT
UNFAIR
INJUSTICE
LIE
HATE
BAD
WRONG
SELF-CENTERED
UNKIND

mindful
of the
Golden Rule

★ thankful for the USA ★

one nation indivisible

THIS LAND IS OUR

IN GOD WE TRUST WE THE PEOPLE

Reflect: For what am I thankful in our country?

Why am I grateful to live here?

GOAL

liberty and justice for all

FREEDOM

RIGHTS

speak
write
meet
protest
worship
vote
run for office
serve on a jury

SERVICES -
Public education, public roads, public libraries
postal service, emergency response
Local, state, national parks, forests, seashores, monuments
Food, drug, health, workplace, environmental, sanitation,
safety regulations

WE THE PEOPLE EQUITY

opportunity

I VOTED

for a practice of gratitude

CPSIA information can be obtained at www.ICGtesting.com
Printed in the USA
LVIW010121040121
675622LV00001B/2